CULTURAL ET

A GUIDE FOR THE
WELL-INTENTIONED

Athena Persephoni Publications

Dedicated to all our relations.

Originally published by Market Wimmin in 1990, with a revised edition published in 1991.

Cover designed by Amoja Three Rivers and Ruth Steinberger. Graphics by Ruth Steinberger.

ISBN-print: 978-1-7335170-0-3

Athena Persephoni Publications
Minneapolis, MN 55411

CONTENTS

ACKNOWLEDGEMENTS AND CREDITS....................VII

I. INTRODUCTION 1

II. DEFINING OURSELVES...2

III. WHAT IS ETHNOCENTRICISM AND..................4
WHAT CAN I TAKE FOR IT?

IV. FOR YOUR INFORMATION 7

V. A FEW LIES LAID BARE 14

VI. JUST DON'T DO THIS. OKAY? 15

VII. SEEING RED...19

VIII. CONTEMPLATIONS...21

IX. TAKING ACTION..26

X. EPILOGUE...28

NOTES...29

ACKNOWLEDGEMENTS and CREDITS

I would like to express my gratitude

To Margarita Benitez
    Judy Chen
    Alix Dobkin
    Fong Hermes
    Carol Hwang
    Lola Lai Jong
    Loba Nemajea
    Billie Potts
    Irenia Quitiquit
    Ruth Segal
    For their suggestions, advice and sisterhood.

To Marie Beaumont and the other women of the Womyn of Color Tent, of the Michigan Womyn's Music Festival, and to all the festival family, for their strength, support and inspiration.

To Sara Lucia Hoagland, for guidance through the Land of Printing and Publishing, and for engineering practicalities.

To Lynn Clark, for help in hard times.

To Blanche Jackson, for enthusiastic and unflagging confidence and support, and for permission to reprint parts of her work, ANTI-RACISM: THE 7-STEP PROGRAM.

And to Thea Elijah and Jodi of Hikáne, for pulling my coat.

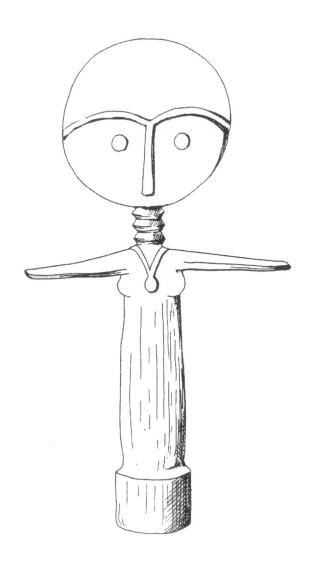

VIII

I. INTRODUCTION

Racism and the racial stereotypes it spawns are so subtly interwoven into the fabric of Western society that very often even those with the best of intentions will display bad cultural manners. This does not necessarily mean one is a bad person. Sometimes people just don't know any better. This guide is to help people avoid some of the obvious as well as not so obvious pitfalls of unwitting racism and anti-Semitism. This does not try to talk anyone out of being racist or anti-Semitic. Rather it seeks to help those with good and righteous intentions to refine behavior and attitudes bred in cultural ignorance.

Cultural Etiquette is intended for people of all "races," nationalities and creeds, not necessarily just "white" people, because no one living in Western society is exempt from the influences of racism, racial stereotypes, race and cultural prejudices and anti-Semitism. I include anti-Semitism in the discussion of racism because it is simply another manifestation of cultural and racial bigotry.

There are many millions of people of color and Jewish people in the world and this guide cannot possibly hope to represent the opinions of each and every one. Its advice and recommendations have come from observations and from the life-experience of the author, who has been a woman of color all her life and expects to remain so, and from interviews with a small but representative group of women of color and Jewish women, all of whom are experts on their own oppression.

II. DEFINING OURSELVES

Racial and cultural designations vary from place to place and, let's face it, are arbitrary to begin with. The following definitions are based upon the cultural alliances prevalent in 20th century U.S.A.

"People of Color" is a term that refers to any people who have other than "white" European ancestry. This includes:
Africans
Asians/Pacific Islanders
Latinas/Latinos
Middle Eastern people
Native Americans
and people of "mixed" ancestry, i.e.: ancestry from any of the above plus white European.

AFRICAN - includes anyone from anywhere on this planet with any African ancestry. Most African people born in the U.S.A. prefer to be called African American rather than "Black" because it strengthens our connection with the Motherland and gives us more of a sense of connection with our own cultures and traditions. Some of us, in acknowledging ourselves to be Africans who were born in America, identify simply as African.

There are African Americans, African-Barbadians, Brazilians, Canadians, Cubans, Nicaraguans, Peruvians, Puerto Ricans, Salvadorans and many other kinds of Africans. There are significant African populations in every country in the Western hemisphere, with the possible exception of Iceland and Greenland. The boats may have dropped us off in different places, but Africa is our Mother and we are all kin.

ASIAN/PACIFIC ISLANDERS - include people indigenous to Australia, Baluchistan, Bangladesh, Bhutan, Burma, Cambodia, China, India, Japan, Java, Korea, Malaysia, Nepal, New Guinea, Pakistan, the Philippines, Thailand, Tibet, Vietnam, and all the islands between the Asian continent and North and South America.

Because the term "Oriental" conjures so many negative stereotypes, people indigenous to the continent of Asia prefer to be called Asians.

LATINAS and LATINOS - (who are people of color) are Spanish-surnamed people, people of Spanish ancestry, and/or people originating from Spanish-speaking countries of the Western hemisphere, the Caribbean Islands, Central and South America, and the U.S.A. who have any African and/or Native ancestries.

MIDDLE EASTERN people of color include Armenian, Arab, Cypriot, Iranian, Iraqi, Jordanian, Kuwati, Lebanese, Palestinian, Syrian, Turkish, Yemenite, and non-European Israeli people.

NATIVE AMERICAN, ALEUT, INUIT people are those who are indigenous to the lands of the Western Hemisphere, i.e.: North, South and Central America and the Caribbean Islands.

III. WHAT IS ETHNOCENTRISM AND WHAT SHOULD I TAKE FOR IT?

Ethnocentrism, according to the Random House Dictionary of the English language, means "a tendency to view alien groups or cultures in terms of one's own" and "the belief in the inherent superiority of one's own group and culture, accompanied by a feeling of contempt for other groups and cultures."

All people are people. It is ethnocentric to use a generic term such as "people" to refer only to white people and then racially label everyone else. This creates and reinforces the assumption that whites are the norm, the real people, and that all others are aberrations, and somehow a bit less than truly human. It is seeing white people as the center and everyone else as variations on the theme.

What function does racial labeling serve? If you're talking about someone, or relating an incident, how necessary is it to mention the race or color of the people involved? What picture are you trying to create? Unless you're making a point that is relevant to the topic of conversation, think about whether you really need to racially label anybody.

"Exotic," when applied to human beings, is ethnocentric and racist. It defines people of color only as we relate to white people. It implies a state of other-ness, or foreign origin, apart from the norm. It is not a compliment.

"Ethnic" refers to nationality or race. Everyone's nationality or race. Margaret Thatcher, Susan B. Anthony and Bach are just as "ethnic" as Miriam Makeba, Indira Gandhi and Johnny Colon.

While it is true that most citizens of the U.S.A. are white, at least 4/5 of the world's population consists of people of color. Therefore, it is statistically incorrect as well as ethnocentric to refer to us as minorities. The term "minority" is used to reinforce the idea of people of color as "other."

TECHNOLOGY and SUPREMACY

Within the cultures of many people, more value is placed on relationships, and on the maintenance of tradition and spirituality, than on the development and acquisition of machinery. It is ethnocentric and racist to apply words like backward, primitive, uncivilized, savage, barbaric, or underdeveloped to people whose technology does not include plumbing, microwaves and microchips. Are people somehow more human or more humane if they have more technological toys?

LITERACY

It is good to be able to read and write. It is good to have a culture that values literacy. It is also good to have cultures that value oral tradition, which is what some people have instead of written traditions. It is a more immediate and personal form of communication and transmission of culture, and it is just as "good" and "smart" as a literate culture. It does not denote "backwardness." It is simply indicative of a worldview that differs from that of the 20th century European.

PROGRESS

Many people of color believe that the ancients who created our cultures and traditions were divinely inspired, and that it is incumbent upon us, even our sacred duty, to try to live up to and maintain their holy ideals. Righteousness may lie in how faithfully we can adhere to the old ways. The concept of "progress" is therefore not of universal value and should never be used as a measurement for judging people's worth.

RELIGION

Monotheism is not more "advanced" than polytheism. It is simply another kind of spirituality, and both have equal validity. The notion of "one true god, one true faith" is often used to invalidate the ancient and complex religious traditions of millions of people.

"Fetish" is a term that means object of spiritual veneration, but in Western society, it is mainly applied to the religious items of people of color in an effort to diminish their depth and importance. One never hears a crucifix referred to as a fetish, even though it basically serves the same purpose as an Acuaba or even the ancient Asherah.

A cult is a particular system of religious worship. If the religious practices of the Yorubas constitute a cult, then so do those of the Methodists, Catholics, and Episcopalians, etc.

The very concept of missionaries presupposes a right vs. wrong scenario: right being Christian, and wrong being any other traditional spirituality. It's perfectly fine to embrace whatever religious faith that inspires you, but it is the height of ethnocentric arrogance to assume that your religion is superior to anyone else's and to try to force it upon them.

There is no up or down in outer space, therefore north as "up" and south as "down" are purely arbitrary designations. The universally familiar picture of Europe and North America being at the top of maps and globes, then, is just a visual device to reinforce the idea that it is right and proper for white people to be on top, to dominate the world. To reorient yourself, rotate maps and globes 180°.

IV. FOR YOUR INFORMATION

A large radio/tape player is a boom-box, or a stereo or a box or a large metallic ham sandwich with speakers. It is not a "ghetto blaster."

Everybody can blush. Everybody can bruise. Everybody can tan and get sunburned. Everybody.

Everybody has "natural rhythm." It is our human birthright. If you don't have perceptual or neuromuscular impairment, and yet you feel unable to perceive or respond to rhythms in any relevant, satisfying or graceful way, then perhaps you may want to examine the personal, cultural and historical paths that led to this unfortunate deficiency. Not having rhythm is not natural.

Judaism is no more patriarchal than any other patriarchal religion.

Koreans are not taking over. Neither are Jews. Neither are the Japanese. Neither are the West Indians. These are myths put out and maintained by the ones who really have. It is a conscious and time-honored tactic for the white, straight, gentile males at the top to create situations in which the rest of us are encouraged to blame each other for our respective oppressions. Don't fall for it.

All hair is "good" hair.

Dreadlocks, locks, dreads, natty dreads, etc., is an ancient traditional way that African people sometimes wear their hair. It is not braided, it is "locked." Locking is the natural tendency of African hair to kit and bond to itself. It locks by itself; we don't have to do anything to it to make it lock. It is permanent; once locked, it cannot come undone. It gets washed just as regularly as anyone else's hair. No, you may not touch it, don't ask.

Dreadlocks is not a style. Usually a person who wears dreads does so as a cultural, spiritual and philosophical expression. It is also an expression of solidarity with other African peoples. Although straight-haired people can dread, it is an expression that uniquely lends itself to the hair of African people.

Not all people with dreadlocks are from Jamaica. Neither are they necessarily Rastafarians. Neither are they drug dealers or "militants."

Not all Jamaicans are Rastafarians.

Not all Rastafarians are Jamaicans.

Native Americans and Native American cultures are alive and thriving, thank you. In fact, you are on our land.

Most African Americans are also Native American. Intermarriage among us has always been extremely common, particularly among the Eastern and Southern nations, and especially during the 17th, 18th, and 19th centuries.

One of the most effective and insidious aspects of racism is cultural genocide. Not only have African Americans been cut off from our African tribal roots, but because of generations of whites pitting African against Indian, and Indian against African, we have been cut off from our Native American roots as well. Consequently, most African Native Americans no longer have tribal affiliations, or even know for certain what people they are from.

Columbus didn't discover diddly-squat. There were millions of Native Americans who have known for countless generations that what they were living on was land, and that where it was—was right here.

Draining the swamps
Clearing the forests
Taming the West
Converting the heathens
Manifest destiny
Noble, suffering pioneers
Intrepid settlers
Brave explorers

are all romanticized, idealized, distorted and dishonest images of what was really a prolonged, unconscionably violent invasion and overthrow of many nations of perfectly good people. And it is still going on.

White people have not always been "white," nor will they always be "white." It is a political alliance. Things will change.

No person of color can be a racist as long as white people maintain power. This is because racism is "power over." A person of color may have race prejudice, but until most of Congress, state, provincial, and local governments, the Pentagon, the FBI, CIA, all major industries, the Stock Exchange, Fortune 500 members, the educational system, health care system, the International Monetary Fund, the armed forces and the police force are all operated and controlled by people of color and their cultural values, we do not have the kind of power that it takes to be racist toward anyone.

Similarly "reverse racism," within the context of present society, is a contradiction in terms.

During slavery, white masters routinely raped African women. This practice was so widespread that there are virtually no African American people who do not have some European ancestry. This is why there is such a wide variation of skin color and hair texture among Africans born in the Americas.

Many people have friends and acquaintances of different backgrounds. The woman of color who is washing the dishes may not be the maid. She could be somebody's overnight guest, washing off her own plate.

Slavery is not a condition unique to African people. In fact, the word "slave" comes from the Slav people of Eastern Europe. Because so many Slavs were enslaved by other people (including Africans) especially in the Middle Ages, their very name came to be synonymous with the condition.

Virtually every human group has been enslaved by some other human group at one time or another.

Native Americans were also enslaved by Europeans. Because it is almost impossible to successfully enslave large numbers of people in their own land, most enslaved Native Americans from the continental U.S. were shipped to Bermuda, and the West Indies, where many intermarried with the Africans.

Middle Eastern women are not necessarily any more oppressed than any other women living under a patriarchy.

The media images we see of poor, miserable, starving, disease-ridden "third world" people of color are distorted and misleading. Nowhere among the tearful appeals for aid do they discuss the conditions that created and continue to create such hopeless poverty. In point of fact, these countries, even after they threw off the stranglehold of colonialism, have been subjected to a constant barrage of resource plundering, political meddling and brutal economic manipulation by European and American interests. Most non-Western countries could function quite adequately and feed themselves quite well if they were permitted political and economic self-determination.

Middle Eastern people embrace may faiths. We can be Muslim, Christian, Jewish, Baha'ist, Zoroastrian, practitioners of other ancient spiritual traditions, atheist, or agnostic.

It is redundant to say "Black African." It is a contradiction in terms to say "white African."

All Africans are Black. Everyone else on the continent of Africa is either a visitor, an invader, or the descendant of invaders. Period.
(From a lecture by Dr. John H. Clarke)

People do not have a hard time because of their race or cultural background. No one is attacked, abused, oppressed, pogromed upon or enslaved because of their race, creed or cultural background. People are attacked, abused, oppressed, pogromed upon or enslaved because of racism and anti-Semitism! There is a subtle but important difference in the focus here. The first implies some inherent fault or shortcomings within the oppressed person or group. The second redirects the responsibility back to the real source of the problem.

The United States is not a Christian country. There are millions of Jews, Muslims, Hindus, and Traditionalists.

The U.S.-Mexican border is itself illegal. Much of the "American" Southwest was stolen from Mexico in 1848, in an unprovoked war of pure imperialism. If anyone is an illegal alien on this continent, it is the European.

One fourth of all the people in the world are Chinese.

The neighborhoods of urban people of color are sometimes run down because of poverty, depression and hopelessness, and the racist behavior of banks, city planners and government and industry. But before anyone again sighs, "There goes the neighborhood," one should consider this: Before white people invaded these lands, the air was clean, the water was pure and the earth was unspoiled.

In 500,000 years of African cultures, we never had a drug problem until we were brought here.

Jewish American Princess or JAP is an anti-Semitic term.

It is not "good luck" to touch the hair of an African American.

Don't assume that people of color in the service industry—maids, housekeepers, chauffeurs, nannies, and mammies—really love and are emotionally loyal to their employers. Once in a while one might hear of a Beulah or Uncle Tom who just dotes on ol' master or young missis, but be assured that these kinds of servants are suffering from a bad case of internalized oppression. And while some real emotional bonding might occasionally transcend this inherently inequitable and exploitive situation, the "love" is usually just an expression of economic expedience. If servants of color had the chance to do something better with their lives, how many do you think would choose to wait on white people? The loving, grinning, selfless, big-tiddied black mammy is part of the ante-bellum, Nigra Mythology that white folks have created to assuage their own guilt.

It is repugnant to people of color for whites to romanticize our oppression and exploitation, such as in the case of
—Asian women's so-called passivity
—the domestic exploitation of people of color within white homes
—"vanishing" Native American cultures
—anybody's poverty
—anybody's pain

Everyone speaks with an accent. Language is a fluid, flexible tool that naturally reflects the life and culture of the speaker, and always changes with the situation. All "accents" and "dialects" are legitimate, proper and equal in value.

Many people of color value and consciously choose to keep their "accents" because it is an affirmation of our respective cultural identities.

Puerto Rico is a commonwealth of the United States. The people of Puerto Rico are full American citizens.

Native American reservations exist as sovereign nations within U.S. borders. Some even issue their own passports.

Most Latinas and Latinos prefer *not* to be called Hispanic.

The term "Banana Republic" trivializes the struggles that Latinas and Latinos have gone through, and still go through to have stable sovereign governments in their own lands. The image of the so-called "Banana Republic" continues to propagate the lie that Latinas and Latinos are hot-blooded, unstable, violent and incapable of competent self-rule, and it deflects attention away from Uncle Sam whose economic and political interests are always behind political upheavals and unrest in South and Central America, and the Caribbean.

People's traditional clothes are not costumes. They are simply clothes.

In the study and discussion of such subjects as anthropology, archeology, sociology and history, there is a lot of double-think when it comes to defining people. At last we cut to the bone of this confusion and present to you:

RACIAL TERMS, DEFINITIONS AND DESIGNATIONS UNVEILED!

Nilotic = Black
Hamitic = Black
Berber = Black
Tuareg = Black
Cushite = Black
Egyptian = Black
proto-Egyptian = Black
pre-dynastic proto-Egyptian = Black
Negroid = Black
Africoid = Black
Eurafrican = Black
brown-skinned Mediterranean = Black
black white people = Black
Abyssinian = Black
Ethiopian = Black
Creole = Black
Afro-Semitic = Black
Afro-Asian = Black
Austroloid = Black
proto-Austroloid = Black
Natufian = Black
Khemetic = Black
Canaanite = Black
Negrito = Black
Grimaldi = Black
Venus of Willendorf = Black
Black-heads of Sumer = Black
Doliocephalic = Black
Steatopygic = Black
African = Black
Black = Black.

V. A FEW LIES LAID BARE

Asians are not "mysterious," "fatalistic," or "inscrutable."

Black people do not have unusually large genitals.

Native Americans are not stoic, mystical or vanishing.

Latin people are no more hot-tempered, hot-blooded or emotional than anyone else. We do not have flashing eyes, teeth or daggers. We are lovers pretty much like other people. Very few of us deal with any kind of drugs.

Middle Easterners are not fanatics, terrorists or all oil rich.

Jewish people are not particularly rich, clannish, or experts in money matters.

Not all African Americans are poor, athletic or ghetto-dwellers.

Most Asians in America are not scientists, mathematicians, geniuses or rich.

Southerners are not any less intelligent than anybody else.

VI. JUST DON'T DO THIS. OKAY?

Do not grab, pat, pull on, feel, caress or touch the hair of a person of color,
—unless you have a personal, equitable relationship with her/him.
—unless you know them well enough to flirt with them.
—unless invited to do so.

All people of color are not extroverted and assertive. Sometimes even if you ask to touch someone's hair, they may give permission because they feel awkward, or do not want to be impolite. Err on the side of sensitivity. Don't touch any stranger's hair, unless invited to do so. And if you are simply beside yourself with curiosity, use it as an opportunity to practice self-restraint. You can center yourself and meditate on the reasons you feel so compelled to put your hands on this other person's hair. Remember, people of color are not specimens or exhibits, and this is not a petting zoo. Touching the hair is considered a very personal thing to many people.

It is not a compliment to tell someone: "I don't think of you as
Jewish
Black
Asian
Latina
Middle Eastern
Native American
Or "I think of you as white."

Do not use a Jewish person or person of color to hear your confession of past racist transgressions. If you have offended a particular person, then apologize to that person. But don't (please don't) just pick some person of color or Jewish person at random, or who is unrelated to the incident, to confess to and beg forgiveness from. Find a priest or a therapist.

Also don't assume that Jews and people of color necessarily want to hear about how prejudiced your Uncle Fred is, no matter now terrible you think he is. It is often painful for us to listen to this type of thing. And why do you want us to join you in putting down your disgusting uncle? Educate him yourself if he is not beyond help. Describing his bigotry to us does no one any good.

Sometimes members of a racial/cultural group will call themselves or each other racially derogatory terms. We may do it in an effort to diffuse or neutralize the pain of racism or anti-Semitism. Or we may use these terms for a private and personal irony. Or we may be expressing our own internalized oppression. Whatever the reason, it's our business and it's up to us to work it out. It is never O.K. for a person who is not of that group to use those racially derogatory terms.

Not even if you're married to or lovers with a person from that group.

No matter how close to that group you feel or how much they seem to accept you.

No matter if they say these racial things in front of you.

Even if individuals from that group tell you it's O.K. to use those terms, that they don't mind, assume that everyone else in the group would still be offended.

If you have occasion to quote another person's racist remark, try to allude to it or just use the first letter of the word, rather than inflict it, however second-hand, on the listening person of color or Jew. It is extremely painful for us to hear others use those terms, no matter what the circumstances.

Do not mimic the language, accent, or mannerisms of Jews or people of color. We are not cartoons.

Don't touch or invade the personal space of a person of color or a Jewish person unless you have established a personal, equitable relationship with them.

If you are white and/or gentile, do not assume that the next Jewish person or person of color you see will feel like discussing this guide with you. Sometimes we get tired of teaching this subject.

It is definitely not O.K. to use terms like "Jew them down" or "Jew town."

Don't say things like, "Gee, you don't look
    Native American
    Black
    Asian
    Jewish
    Latina
    Middle Eastern.

Please don't go around expecting you can be part of another ethnic group now because you feel you were of that group "in a former life."

If you are white, don't brag to a person of color about your overseas trip to our homeland. Especially when we cannot afford such a trip. Similarly, don't assume that we are overjoyed to see the expensive artifacts that you brought back.

If you are not Jewish, please don't wear the Star of David as a fashion statement.

Works like "gestapo," "concentration camp" and "Hitler" are only appropriate when used in reference to the Holocaust. These terms can be extremely painful for a Jew to hear and should not be used casually.

Do not equate bad, depressing or negative things with darkness. Observe how language reflects racism:
    A black mood
    A dark day
    A black heart.

The meaning of the word denigrate is to demean by darkening. Be creative. There's thousands of adjectives in the English language that do not equate evil with the way people of color look. How about instead of "the pot calling the kettle black" you say, "the pus calling the maggot white"? Think of and use positive dark and black imagery. Dark can be rich and deep and cool and sweet. Black is a sacred color in many religious traditions. Next time you see a priest or a nun, check out the colors they're wearing.

Don't assume that it is O.K. to ask people of color about their racial background. While some might prefer to be questioned, many consider it extremely rude. Be sensitive and use your judgement.

Never, ever ask any person of color:
"Why are you so light-skinned?"
"Why is your hair so straight?"
"Why is your hair so light?"
"Why are your eyes so light?"
"Why aren't your eyes slanted?"

Musical instruments such as drums, rattles and shekeres have strong spirits and when they belong to other people should not be handled casually. Never touch another person's instrument without asking permission and do not take it personally if they say "no." Also, do not keep asking in the hopes that the instrument's owner will eventually change her mind. She might, after she gets to know you better, but pestering is the wrong thing to do. If you own a drum, rattle, shekere or other instrument with a spirit, it's O.K. to politely turn down someone's request to hold it or borrow it, if it does not feel quite right to you.

All human beings are equal. No one is "better" than anyone else. No human being, of any color, however poor, deprived or uneducated is "trash," and should never be referred to as such.

VII. SEEING RED

Malignment and trivialization of Native Americans and our cultures has become so casual, commonplace and acceptable that it can sometimes be difficult for non-Indians to see the racism embedded in many time-honored elements of American culture.

"Indian giver"—what exactly does that mean?

Someone who would give you something and then later take it back?

Like when the U.S. "gave" Indians land and then took it back?

An untrustworthy person who does not honor agreements?

Like when the U.S. government reneged on almost every treaty they ever negotiated with Native Americans?

If we had to characterize a group by these traits, then perhaps a more appropriate term would be "white giver."

It is disrespectful, culturally demeaning and insulting to call sports teams by such names as "Indians," "Redskins" and "Braves." It is as unacceptable to us as the names

"Pittsburg Pollacks"

"Harrisburg Honkies" or

"New York Negroes" would be to non-Indians.

It is also culturally demeaning to turn sacred and serious elements of various Native American cultures into team chants, cheers and other assorted sports rituals. Just imagine if the situation were somehow reversed. There might be the "Washington Popes" with the chalice and cross as official insignias. Perhaps during half-time the cheerleaders could do a choreographed crucifixion of a collegiate Jesus mascot. Instead of the tomahawk chop, "Pope" fans could chant something that sounded a little like "Amazing Grace" while shooting into the air with "holy water" pistols.

If you are wincing, cringing, getting steamed or offended, then you are starting to know how *we* feel when we witness the constant, ongoing trivialization of Native American cultures.

Many non-Indians profess love and respect for our "nobleness." But almost worse than the insults is the insensitivity of those who care more about their fantasies of who they want Native Americans to be than they care about the real needs and wishes of living, breathing Native Americans.

Native Americans are not getting more privilege than non-Indians when they exercise certain fishing or hunting rights. These are *rights* guaranteed by treaties between sovereign nations, and the terms are entitled to the same observance, enforcement and respect as any other international laws.

It is an ironic twist of legislative and ethical double-think that

Theft and fraud are illegal and immoral, and punishable by law.

To knowingly accept goods obtained by theft or fraud is illegal, immoral and punishable by law.

And by law, the illegally obtained goods must be returned to their rightful owners.

However,

Even though most of North, South and Central America and the Caribbean islands were taken from Native peoples by force and by fraud, virtually no European invader has ever been punished for it.

And even though it has become fashionable to sadly and openly admit that these lands were obtained illegally,

Who is working to right these moral wrongs? Who is returning these stolen properties to their rightful "owners"?

VIII. CONTEMPLATIONS

Do you have friends or acquaintances who are really terrific except they're really racist? If you quietly accept that part of them, you are giving their racism tacit approval.

As an exercise, pretend you are from another planet and you want examples of typical human beings for your photo album. Having never heard of racism, you'd probably pick someone who represents the majority of the people on the planet—an Asian woman.

How many is too many? We have heard well-meaning liberals say things like "This event is too white. We need more people of color." Well, how many more do you need? Fifty? A hundred? What percentage of people of color should a festival, a conference, a party, an organization or a neighborhood be? Twenty percent? Fifty percent? What if the result of enthusiastic outreach made an event or locale seventy-five percent persons of color? Ninety percent? Would this be more than you need? Just what is your standard for personal racial comfort?

African drumming and dancing is not an occasion that calls for the abandonment of all control and reason, nor is it an invitation to act "savage" or "wild." African polyrhythms are extremely complex and precise and are deeply rooted in ancient spiritual traditions. It is not a free-for-all. The drummers and dancers watch, listen, and respond to each other in an improvised, but structured exchange. When it is on the stage, African drumming and dancing can be entertainment, but under most other circumstances it is ritual, or spiritual exploration, or a private conversation and not necessarily open for public input. If you are a white person, and you happen upon people of color drumming and dancing, and you want to join in but you don't know if you should or not, use these unclear occasions as opportunities for meditation and centering. Relax. Breathe. It's O.K. for you not to be in the center of everything you see. People of color sometimes need to have the time and space to explore our heritage and traditions—for ourselves and by ourselves. This does not necessarily mean that you must go away. It does mean that at such times we usually prefer that white people maintain an outer circle as allies and observers, rather than spontaneous and uninvited participants. It's fine to be patient, be still, and just listen.

When you do have an opportunity to play an African instrument, it is a good idea to learn the proper techniques for playing it, just as you would with a violin or piano. Just banging away and playing "what you feel" won't do.

Only Africans and their descendants can be African drummers. If you are not an African, playing African drums will not make you an African drummer.

It is not O.K. to try to sell Native American spiritualties. Many traditional Native Americans also feel it is wrong to sell such things as sage, cedar and tobacco.

It is offensive and depressing for people of color to watch aspects of our ancient cultures and traditions become fads and fashions.

People of color and Jewish people have been so all their lives. Further, if we have been raised in a place where white gentiles predominate, then we have been subjected to racism/anti-Semitism all of our lives. We are therefore experts on our own lives and conditions. If you do not understand or believe or agree with what someone is saying about their own oppression, do not automatically assume that they are wrong or paranoid or over-sensitive. Racism and anti-Semitism can be blatant and crude, but it can also be so cunning or insidious that it is often hard to pin it down. It can be as subtle as body language, a look or a vibe. Oppressed people survive by learning to trust their instincts. The well-meaning, (relatively) non-oppressed should follow our lead.

African Native Americans have every right to claim and honor their African ancestors and their Native American ancestors.

It is not "racism in reverse" or "segregation" for Jews or people of color to come together in affinity groups for mutual support. Sometimes we need some time and space apart from the dominant group just to relax and be ourselves. It's like family time. Most of the

U.S.A. is white and gentile with white, gentile rules and values prevailing. Sometimes we need to be in control of our own space, time and values, to shape our own reality on our own turf. Sometimes we need to be alone to commiserate with each other about racism and anti-Semitism, and to formulate plans and strategies for dealing with it. Sometimes we need time and space to explore who we are, free from outsider definitions, influences and ethnocentric imagery. Sometimes we just need an environment that is totally free from even the possibility of racism and anti-Semitism. So when you see: "Asian Women Only," "Jewish Caucus," "Womyn of Color Tent," "Middle Eastern Discussion Group," "Native American Conference," "Open to Latinas," please know that we are not being against anybody by being for ourselves.

If people coming together for group support makes you feel excluded, perhaps there's something missing in your own life or cultural connections.

Why, in most Science Fiction, no matter how many years you go into the future, or how many light years you go out in space, is everyone always white?!?

The various cultures of people of color often seem very attractive to white people. (Yes, we are wonderful, we can't deny it.) But white people should not make a playground out of other people's cultures. We are not quaint. We are not exotic. We are not cool. Our music, art and spiritualties are but small, isolated parts of integrated and meaningful ancient traditions. They were developed within each group, for that group, by the deities and teachers of that group, according to their own particular conditions and connections to the cosmos, and their own particular histories and philosophies. In addition, our cultural expressions carry all the pain, joy, bitterness and hope that reflect our lives and our struggles in dealing with so-called Western civilization. While most philosophies can have universal application, it has been the habit of many non-people of color to select unconnected pieces of our cultures for fads and fashions, taking them totally out of context and robbing them of all meaning and power.

It's like we take all the beautiful old things from our own cultures.

And we take the shit and blood and pain that whites have heaped
upon us too,
And we deal with all of that,
Mix it up,
Compost it,
Plow it under,
Work the soil,
Pull the weeds,
Nurture the seedlings
And finally
Here it is, our garden,
These fruits,
These songs and dances,
These visions.
Then here YOU come,
Fresh from the Big House,
Having neither sowed nor plowed,
But fully expecting to reap.

Now it is perfectly natural for human beings to share and blend
cultures, but let us face a hard reality: 20th century white society is
culturally addicted to exploitation. Cultivate an awareness of your
own personal motivations. Do not simply take and consume. If you
are white and you find yourself drawn to Native American
spirituality, Middle Eastern religion, African drumming, Asian
philosophies, or Latin rhythms, make an effort to maintain some kind
of balance. Don't just learn the fun and exciting things about us and
then go home to your safe, isolated, white, privileged life. Learn about
the history of the people whose culture you're dabbling in. Learn how
our history relates to your own, how your privilege connects and
contributes to our oppression and exploitation. And most importantly,
make it a fair exchange—give something back.

If you want to pick the fruit, then carry some manure and plow
some fields. Give your land back to the Indians and the Mexicans.
Make reparations to the Africans. Work for Native peoples' autonomy
and Puerto Rican independence. Send relief money to Middle Eastern
and Asian disaster victims. Lobby Congress for fair immigration laws.
Provide rides for Elders of color or single mothers who need to get to

the market. Quietly contribute money to the African National Congress, Akwesasne Notes and La Raza. Then take your drum lesson and your dance class. Then burn your sage and cedar.

Sometimes white people who are drawn to other people's cultures are hungry for a way of life with more depth and meaning than what we find in 20th century Western society. Don't forget that every white person alive today is also descended from tribal peoples. If you are white, don't neglect your own ancient traditions. They are as valid as anybody else's, and the ways of your own ancestors need to be honored, remembered and carried on into the future.

"Race" is an arbitrary and meaningless concept. Races among humans don't exist. If there ever was any such thing as race (which there isn't), there has been so much constant crisscrossing of genes for the last 500,000 years that it would have lost all meaning anyway. There are no real divisions between us, only a continuum of variations that constantly change, as we come together and separate according to the flow and movement of human populations.

Racism is a disease that has killed more people than AIDS.

Racism requires attention and energy on the part of the oppressor to keep it in place. Therefore, oppressors are frequently too busy applying racism to attend to matters affecting their own spiritual and cultural well-being and survival.

The successful marketing of racism and other isms is greatly facilitated by early programming for extremely sloppy thinking that passes under the guise of "education."

Anyone who functions in what is referred to as the "civilized" world is a carrier of the disease of racism.

IX. TAKING ACTION

So now that you have acquired all these manners, what do you do with them?

Develop a private pride in the depth of one's intellect:
—by non-institutional self-education.
—by making a regular practice of learning about things that don't seem to have direct bearing on your day-to-day life.

Develop purity of heart. If you can't clearly and openly express what you're thinking, question the validity of what you're thinking.

Collect and experiment with all available tools and techniques for gaining insight.

Practice the ones that are the most challenging, for they carry the greatest and deepest rewards.

Seek tools and techniques for gaining insight that are not readily available. Practice the ones that are the most challenging for the greatest benefits.

Examine what you regard as your own culture as if you were a complete stranger to it. If this proves difficult, find a few people who do not share your values. Ask them to describe your culture to you. Keep quiet and pay attention. Privately imagine yourself to be someone who considers herself different from you. Spend a day seeing the world as they do.

Assume that other people know more about their own lives and cultures than you do.

(From Blanche Jackson's Anti-Racism: The 7-Step Program)

Be an active ally to all oppressed people. Take the initiative in intercepting oppression.

Do not let anyone be racist or anti-Semitic or racially prejudiced in your face.

Have the courage and commitment to lovingly confront even your friends and your employers when they are offensive.

Write letters to the editor.

Support farmworkers by boycotting produce from offending companies.

Do outreach.

Stand up for what you know is right.

Seek out or start anti-racism groups in your community.
Read books by and about people of color and Jewish people.
Treasure your own good heart and good intentions.
Don't expect anti-racism work to always be easy.
Don't be afraid of pain and discomfort.
And don't be afraid to grow.

X. EPILOGUE

Does reading this guide make you uncomfortable? Angry? Confused? Are you taking it personally? Well, not to fret. Racism has created a big horrible mess, and racial healing can sometimes be painful. Just remember that Jews and people of color do not want or need anybody's guilt. We just want people to accept responsibility when it is appropriate, and actively work for change.

Above all, keep this in your mind and in your heart: We are all children of the Great Spirit. As spiritual and physical beings we are the manifestation of the Goddess's effort to know Herself. We are separate and different, yet we come from the same mother, spiritually and biologically, and share the same wonderful life source. Our ultimate challenge and our ultimate goal is to love and nurture one another and all things in creation. Peace and love to all the children of the Earth.

NOTES

For more information about *Cultural Etiquette* and Amoja Three Rivers, go to:

• Cultural Etiquette on Facebook:
https://www.facebook.com/pg/Cultural-Etiquette-A-Guide-for-the-Well-Intentioned-1425427397783664

• Remembering Amoja Three Rivers on Facebook:
https://www.facebook.com/amoja3rivers

• Amoja Three Rivers on Goodreads:
https://www.goodreads.com/author/show/1927508.Amoja_Three_Rivers

• Amoja Three Rivers on Smashwords
https://www.smashwords.com/profile/view/amoja3rivers

Made in the USA
Monee, IL
17 September 2020